How Fighter Pilots
Use Math

By Mary Hense

**Math Curriculum Consultant: Rhea A. Stewart, M.A.,
Specialist in Mathematics, Science,
and Technology Education**

CHELSEA
CLUBHOUSE
An Imprint of Chelsea House Publishers

Math in the Real World: How Fighter Pilots Use Math

Chelsea Clubhouse
An imprint of Chelsea House Publishers
132 West 31st Street
New York NY 10001

Library of Congress Cataloging-in-Publication Data
Hense, Mary.
        How fighter pilots use math / by Mary Hense; math curriculum consultant, Rhea A. Stewart.
              p. cm. — (Math in the real world)
        Includes index.
        ISBN 978-1-60413-605-0
        1. Mathematics—Juvenile literature. 2. Aeronautics—Mathematics—Juvenile literature.
        3. Fighter pilots—Juvenile literature. I. Title. II. Series.
    QA135.6.H46 2010
    510—dc22   2009020242

Chelsea Clubhouse books are available at special discounts when purchased in bulk quantities for businesses, associations, institutions, or sales promotions. Please call our Special Sales Department in New York at (212) 967-8800 or (800) 322-8755.

You can find Chelsea Clubhouse on the World Wide Web at http://www.chelseahouse.com

Developed for Chelsea House by RJF Publishing LLC (www.RJFpublishing.com)
Text and cover design by Tammy West/Westgraphix LLC
Illustrations by Spectrum Creative Inc.
Photo research by Edward A. Thomas
Index by Nila Glikin

Photo Credits: 4: F-35 Joint Strike Fighter Program; 6: U.S. Air Force photo/Staff Sgt. Jake Richmond; 8: VSI Vision Systems International, LLC; 10: U.S. Air Force photo/Airman 1st Class Rachel A. Kocin; school bus: iStockphoto; 12, 14, 16, 20, 27: Courtesy of Lockheed Martin; 18: U.S. Air Force photo/ 2nd Lt. Emily Chilson; 21: U.S. Air Force; 22: iStockphoto.

Printed and bound in the United States of America

Bang RJF 10 9 8 7 6 5 4 3 2 1

This book is printed on acid-free paper.

All links and Web addresses were checked and verified to be correct at the time of publication. Because of the dynamic nature of the Web, some addresses and links may have changed since publication and may no longer be valid.

Table of Contents

Answers and helpful hints for the You Do the Math
activities are in the Answer Key.

Words that are defined in the Glossary are
in **bold** type the first time they appear in the text.

Air Acrobatics

The jet engine roars as Colonel Maria Sanchez races the F-35 down the runway. The plane leaps into the air. At 1,000 feet, she banks and circles the Air Force base to give three other fighter planes time to take off and join her.

Sanchez heads north. The three other planes fall into formation around her. Together, the planes make a formation that looks like a trapezoid in the sky.

Sanchez's plan is to land at a base that is 675 miles away. Sanchez and the others accelerate to 700 miles per hour. They climb to 30,000 feet. Sanchez estimates they'll be at the base in less than an hour.

An F-35 (on the left in the photo) in the air during a test flight.

Missile Alert

Over the radio Sanchez hears an alert from the pilot of the plane located at 8 o'clock. A ground-to-air missile is headed her way.

Colonel Sanchez climbs at 80 degrees to 40,000 feet. The missile follows her plane. She rotates the aircraft into a backward summersault and dives nose first. She glimpses the missile at 11 o'clock. It's going to miss her.

She pulls out of the dive, banking 90 degrees to the right. She feels a 9 G force press her into her seat through the sharp turn. She levels the plane.

Colonel Sanchez laughs when she hears the pilots on the radio agree on her new nickname: The Air Acrobat.

You Do the Math

Clock Locations

Pilots talk to each other about their locations and the locations of objects around them. Pilots describe locations as if they were in the middle of a clock face.

Pilots say that a storm cloud to their right is at 3 o'clock. A mountain straight ahead is at 12 o'clock. Use the clock face above. Describe the location of an aircraft flying right behind you.

Fighter Pilot Gear

Wearing her G-suit, this pilot climbs out of an F-16 fighter after a training flight.

Fighter pilots wear G-suits to lessen the effects of **G forces**. G forces describe how heavy a person feels. Someone standing still on the ground feels a force of 1 G. You might feel a greater number of G's when your elevator suddenly rises or when you spin on a theme park ride.

G forces can cause blood to move away from a pilot's head. The pilot could get dizzy and faint. The G-suit inflates around the pilot's legs and body. The tightness prevents blood from pooling below the chest.

Pilots wear survival vests over their G-suits. These vests contain everything pilots need if they have to eject. When a pilot ejects, the pilot's seat shoots out of the cockpit like a rocket. The pilot then parachutes to safety.

The survival vest has objects for alerting rescuers: a radio, **beacon**, whistle, and **strobe light** and a flare that can make a smoke trail 1,250 feet high. It has objects for finding location: a **compass** and a GPS (global positioning system) device.

Different G Forces

With a G force of 0, or 0 times your body weight, you feel weightless. With a G force of 1, or 1 times your body weight, you feel normal. With a G force of 2, or 2 times your body weight, you feel twice as heavy. The table below shows how many G's you might feel doing different things.

You Do the Math

How Much Is 9 G?

When Colonel Sanchez banked her fighter, she felt a G force of 9. Look at the table. How many times greater is that G force than a roller coaster's G force?

How G Forces Feel		
G Forces	**How Heavy You Feel (w = your weight)**	**What You Might Be Doing**
0 G	0 x w	floating in a space station
1 G	1 x w	reading a book
3 G	3 x w	riding on a roller coaster
5 G	5 x w	cornering in a fast race car
9 G	9 x w	turning in a fighter plane

Helmets and Cockpits

Fighter pilots' helmets protect pilots' heads and deliver oxygen for breathing. The helmets have radios for talking to people on the ground and in the air.

Helmets made for the F-35 fighter can do much more than that. Projectors on the helmet show information and pictures on the **visor**. Cameras around the outside of the plane send pictures to the projectors. The information and pictures help the pilot to know what's going on around the aircraft.

Information and pictures from cameras around the outside of the plane are shown on an F-35 pilot's visor.

Inside the Cockpit

Most fighter planes have single-pilot cockpits. The pilot's seat tilts back at an angle so that many of the G forces are **perpendicular**, or at a **right angle**, to the pilot's spine. The seat angle reduces the number of G-force injuries. The seat has a seatbelt and a harness for safety.

The pilot's instrument panel has voice control. That makes it easy for a pilot to do things like change the radio channel during a 9-G turn. Instead of lifting an arm that feels like it weighs 90 pounds, the pilot can just tell the instruments to change the channel.

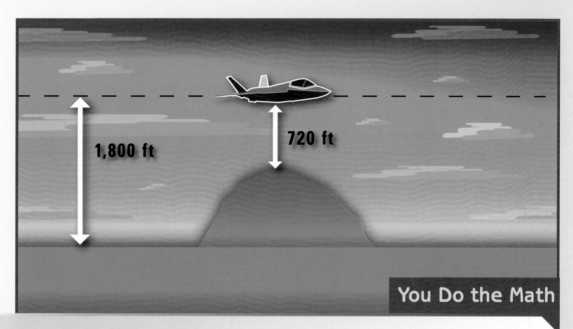

1,800 ft

720 ft

You Do the Math

How High Is That Hill?

Instrument panels have **altimeters**, or instruments that tell pilots how high they are flying. The pressure altimeter works by measuring air pressure outside of the jet. As a jet climbs, the air pressure decreases. The pressure altimeter uses air pressure data to display the jet's **altitude**, or distance above sea level, in feet.

When pilots fly near the ground, they need to know how far they are from objects, such as mountain tops, towers, and buildings. Pilots use **radar** altimeters to measure **height**, or distance above objects on Earth's surface.

Suppose a pilot is above a hill. The pressure altimeter shows an altitude of 1,800 feet. The radar altimeter shows a height of 720 feet. How tall is the hill?

Expensive Machines

Through training and practice, pilots know what their planes can and cannot do. They know how to make the planes perform well.

Fighter pilots on a mission sometimes must do risky things. At other times, pilots are careful not to risk damaging their planes. They know that their planes are expensive. One fighter plane can cost about as much as 2,000 school buses!

In 2009, you could buy one F-22 Raptor (above) for about $142,000,000 and one school bus for about $71,000.

How Expensive Are Missiles?

The F-22 Raptor jet can carry two types of missiles, Sidewinders and Slammers.

Sidewinder missiles seek out targets that give off heat, such as the jet engines of enemy planes. Up to six Sidewinders can fit into a Raptor.

Slammer missiles use radar to find targets. They can travel for up to 20 miles and travel at **supersonic** speeds, or speeds greater than the speed of sound. Six Slammers can fit into a Raptor.

Both types of missiles are expensive, but one Slammer missile costs between 4 and 5 times as much as one Sidewinder. The table below shows the measurements and cost of each kind of missile: Sidewinders and Slammers.

You Do the Math

Buying Slammers

Use the table. How much would the Air Force have to spend to buy six Slammer missiles?

F-22 Raptor Missiles				
Missile	Length (feet)	Diameter (inches)	Weight (pounds)	Cost (in 2009)
Slammer	12	7	335	$386,000
Sidewinder	$9\frac{5}{12}$	5	190	$ 84,000

Air Force Fighter Planes

One way to lower the cost of one fighter plane is to build many of that kind of fighter plane.

With that in mind, plane builders developed the F-35 Lightning II Joint Strike Fighter. With a few modifications, the Air Force, Marines, and Navy could use the same plane. Before there were F-35s, there were different types of planes for different military branches.

Air Force pilots need planes that go fast, travel far, and are **agile**, or easy to turn. Air Force pilots need planes that use regular runways for take-off and landing.

The F-35A does all of those things. The list on page 13 shows data about this Air Force plane.

An Air Force F-35A on a test flight.

Air Force F-35A

Conventional Take-Off and Landing

Length: 51.5 feet
Wingspan: 35 feet
Wing area: 460 square feet
Weight: 29,300 pounds
Combat radius: about 700 miles
Range: about 1,730 miles

Range and Combat Radius

In the data about the F-35A, the range is the total distance the plane can fly before it runs out of fuel. The combat **radius** is the distance the F-35A can fly before it has to turn back to return to its base for fuel. Why is it called a combat *radius*? Look at the pictures to the right.

Suppose a point on a map is an Air Force base. You can draw line segments from the point to show some of the possible flight paths.

The more flight paths you draw, the more the line segments look like spokes on a wheel.

Eventually the drawing looks like a circle. Each combat radius is a radius of the circle.

You Do the Math

Comparing Range and Combat Radius

Look again at the data about the F-35A. How do the numbers of miles of the range and the combat radius compare?

Marine Fighter Planes

Marine fighter pilots don't have to fly as far as Air Force pilots do. Marines are close to the action. They might be in rugged **terrain** near enemy lines where the best runway is a rough road.

Marine fighter pilots need a plane that can take off within a short distance. They need an aircraft that can land vertically—that is, it can come straight down like a helicopter.

The Marine Corps's F-35B looks just like the Air Force's F-35A. But it can **hover**, or appear to float in one place. It can land vertically just about anywhere.

An F-35B takes off for a test flight.

The F-35B has a range of about 1,240 miles. That's about 490 miles less than the Air Force F-35A's range. But Marine pilots don't need as much distance as Air Force pilots do. The list below shows data about the F-35B.

Marine Corps F-35B

Short Take-Off, Vertical Landing

Length:	51.3 feet
Wingspan:	35 feet
Wing area:	460 square feet
Weight:	32,000 pounds
Combat radius:	about 600 miles
Range:	about 1,240 miles

Rotating Engine

The F-35B can land vertically because its engine rotates, or turns, 90 degrees. The picture to the right shows a 90-degree rotation. When the engine is parallel to the ground, the jet goes forward. When it is perpendicular to the ground, the jet goes up and down.

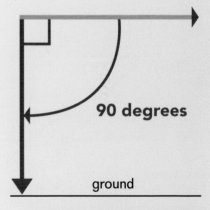

90 degrees

ground

You Do the Math

Learning About Rotation

Draw a picture that shows a 90-degree rotation. First, trace an object, such as a pair of scissors. Next, rotate that object 90 degrees around a point on the object. Then, trace it again.

Navy Fighter Planes

Navy pilots often take off from and land on a ship called an **aircraft carrier**. The runway on an aircraft carrier is short. To get a plane to take-off speed, a **catapult** flings it forward. The carrier runway is also too short for pilots to make the kind of landing they could at an airport.

Most fighter jets need a runway that is at least 7,500 feet long. The largest aircraft carrier is about one-seventh that length. Carrier pilots must stop their planes quickly by hooking onto a wire that stretches across the deck. There are typically 4 parallel wires about 50 feet apart. Pilots try to catch the third wire. If they do, the pilots know they came in neither too high nor too low, but at just the right angle.

The illustration shows an F-35C that has just taken off from an aircraft carrier.

Strong Gear, Large Wings

A Navy fighter plane must be sturdy enough to be shot by a catapult and snagged by a wire. It needs big wings to be able to land in an exact location.

The F-35C fills all those needs. The F-35C's body and landing gear are strong. Its greater wing and tail areas provide more **lift** when the plane approaches a carrier at low speeds. Lift is a force that moves a plane upward when it moves through air. The F-35C has larger flaps and tail slats that make the jet easier to handle. Together, the added lift and improved handling help a pilot steer the F-35C to a wire on the aircraft carrier deck.

The list below shows data about the F-35C.

Navy F-35C

Carrier Take-Off and Landing

Length:	51.4 feet
Wingspan:	43 feet
Wing area:	668 square feet
Weight:	29,300 pounds
Combat radius:	about 750 miles
Range:	about 1,780 miles

You Do the Math

Catapulted Forward How Far?

The pilot feels 4 G when the catapult shoots the plane 290 yards in $1\frac{1}{2}$ seconds. Is that distance closer to 500 feet or 1,000 feet? (Hint: There are 3 feet in 1 yard.)

Fueling an Aircraft

Fueling an aircraft isn't as simple as filling up the tank in a family's car. Fuel adds weight. The more weight an aircraft has, the faster the aircraft burns the fuel.

A pilot uses calculations and charts to find the right amount of fuel for a mission. First, the pilot adds the weights of the payload, or objects the plane carries, such as

An Air Force plane takes on fuel before a flight.

cargo, people, and weapons. Then, the pilot uses a chart to determine how winds, distance, and speed affect the amount of fuel needed for the mission.

Adding Extra Fuel

Even when the pilot's math calculations are exact, the answer, the amount of fuel to take on, is actually an estimate. The pilot then adds an extra amount of fuel to the total. The extra fuel is added to try to make sure the pilot has enough fuel in case conditions change or the mission changes. For example, the weather might change for the worse. Or perhaps the pilot will have to circle the airbase before landing at the end of the mission. Or perhaps the pilot will learn during the mission that the plane will have to go to a different destination because of new plans.

Also, pilots need enough fuel to taxi the plane to the **hangar** after landing. They don't want to complete a mission successfully and then run out of fuel before parking the plane!

You Do the Math

How Many Gallons?

The Air Force's F-35A can hold 18,000 pounds of fuel. A gallon of fuel weighs 6 pounds. How many gallons of fuel can the F-35A hold?

In-Flight Fueling

On some missions, pilots don't stop at airbases for jet fuel. The fuel comes to them.

The KC-135 Stratotanker is a flying service station. It is used to refuel fighters and other planes while they are in the air. A Stratotanker can carry 200,000 pounds of **transfer fuel**, or fuel for other planes.

A pilot and copilot fly the Stratotanker. A boom operator does the fueling. The boom is the tube that fuel runs through from the tanker plane to the fighter plane.

An F-35 takes on fuel from a KC-135.

boom

"Parked" in the Sky

When a jet fighter pilot needs to refuel, the pilot flies the jet beneath the tail of the Stratotanker. The fighter plane looks as if it is parked in the sky. Really, the Stratotanker and the fighter are flying at the same speed.

The boom operator then guides the boom to the waiting aircraft. When the fighter jet has enough fuel, the boom operator moves the boom out of the way. The fighter pilot slows the plane to get out from under the Stratotanker and then flies away.

This is the view a KC-135 boom operator gets when refueling a plane in the air.

You Do the Math

Refueling Time

A KC-135 Stratotanker can pump 6,500 pounds of fuel in a minute. At that rate how many minutes would it take to fill a fighter plane that needs 13,000 pounds of fuel?

Supersonic

$\mathbf{F}$ ighter planes can fly at superson-ic speeds, or speeds faster than the speed of sound. When a plane travels faster than sound, air around the aircraft compresses and changes density. The result can be a pair of loud booms called **sonic booms**.

How fast is the speed of sound? That depends on the density of air. Sound travels faster in denser air. Close to Earth, the air is the densest.

At sea level, the speed of sound is 761 miles per hour. To travel at a supersonic speed at sea level, you have to travel faster than that.

A jet can have a halo around it when it's flying at supersonic speed.

Mach Numbers

Sometimes pi-lots refer to the speed of sound as **Mach** 1. Super-sonic speeds are speeds greater than Mach 1. Mach is a ratio of an aircraft's speed to the speed of sound. Pilots can find the Mach number for their speed by writing a fraction:

$$\frac{\text{speed of aircraft}}{\text{speed of sound}}$$

If the numerator of the fraction is greater than the denominator, then the pilot has a fraction that is greater than 1, and the plane is flying at supersonic speed.

F-35s can fly at Mach 1.6, or about 1,200 miles per hour.

You Do the Math

Is Your Speed Supersonic?

The table shows the speed of sound at different altitudes.

Speed of Sound at Different Altitudes	
Altitude (in feet)	Speed of Sound (in miles per hour)
sea level	761
10,000	734
20,000	707
30,000	678
40,000	660
50,000	660

Would you be traveling at a supersonic speed if you were flying at 700 miles per hour at 20,000 feet? How do you know? If you kept the same speed but climbed to 30,000 feet, would you be traveling at supersonic speed then?

Stealth

Fighter planes are **stealthy**, or hard for enemies to detect. The planes have quiet engines. The color of the planes helps them to blend in with the sky. The planes don't make white streaks in the sky.

Enemies try to spot fighter planes by using radar. Radar equipment sends out radio waves. Radio waves can bounce off a jet, like a basketball bounces off a wall. When the radio waves bounce back to an enemy, the enemy sees the fighter plane on a radar screen.

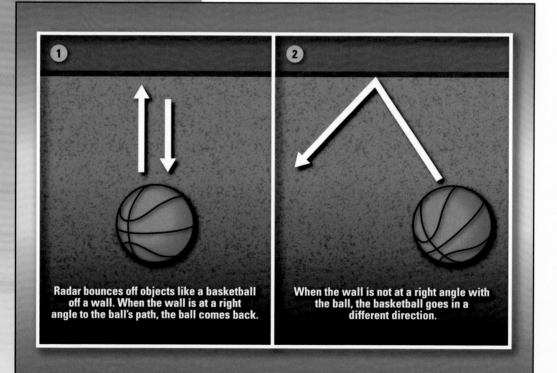

1
Radar bounces off objects like a basketball off a wall. When the wall is at a right angle to the ball's path, the ball comes back.

2
When the wall is not at a right angle with the ball, the basketball goes in a different direction.

Fooling the Radar

Can fighter pilots outrun radio waves? Pilots can rip through the sky as fast as 1,200 miles per hour. Radio waves travel at 186,000 miles per second! At that speed, radio waves could travel to the moon and back in less than 3 seconds.

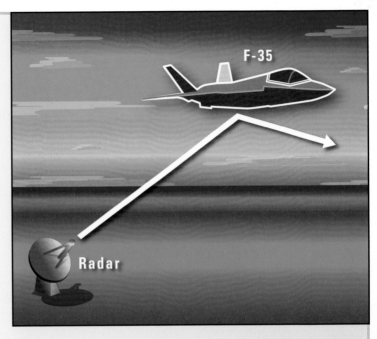

The curves and angles of the F-35 make it stealthy.

A fighter pilot can't outrun radio waves. But the fighter plane's design can prevent radio waves from returning to the enemy. The plane has a special coating that absorbs some radio waves. Also, the plane has specially curved surfaces and angles that cause radio waves to bounce off in different directions. The waves don't bounce back in the direction they came from. This means that the radio waves that are sent out will not return to the enemy's radar receiver.

You Do the Math

Imagine You Have Radar

Suppose that you were equipped with radar. Look around you. Which surfaces would bounce your radio waves back to you?

Navigation

A fighter pilot uses a tool called a compass for finding direction. The compass's face is a circle divided into 360 degrees, as shown in the illustration to the left. North is 0 degrees or 360 degrees. East is 90 degrees. South is 180 degrees. When a pilot's compass points to 225, the pilot is flying to the southwest.

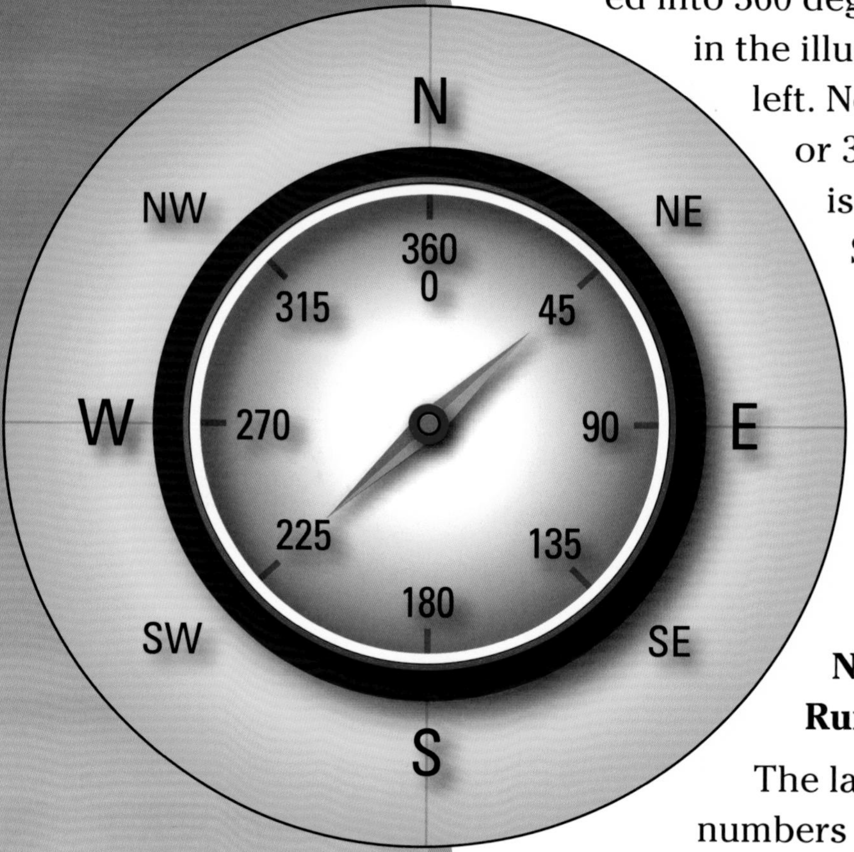

Numbering Runways

The large painted numbers on the ends of runways stand for degrees on a compass. Airbases and airports abbreviate degrees as one-digit or two-digit numbers. The rule is to round the degrees to the nearest ten and drop the ones digit. The table on page 27 shows examples of how this is done.

Writing Degrees Using Runway Abbreviations		
Compass Reading	Round to the Nearest 10	Drop the Ones Digit
48 degrees	50	5
123 degrees	120	12
6 degrees	10	1

From above, a pilot seeing a runway numbered 9 and 27 knows that it runs east-west from 90 degrees to 270 degrees. The numbered runway is a giant navigation tool.

An F-35 pilot brings the plane down on a numbered runway.

The runway numbers give runways their names. A voice from the control tower might direct a pilot to land on Runway 9-27.

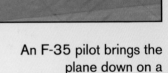

What Are Nautical Miles?

Pilots use **nautical miles** as units for measuring distance. One nautical mile is a unit that represents a fraction of the **circumference** of Earth. Like a compass, Earth's circumference has 360 degrees. Each degree has 60 equal parts called minutes. One minute is one nautical mile.

One nautical mile is about 6,080 feet, or 1.15 standard (statute) miles. Which would be the greater distance, 1,000 nautical miles or 1,000 standard miles? How do you know?

If You Want to Be a Fighter Pilot

Fighter pilots are a small, elite group. In 2008, only four out of every 100 people in the Air Force were pilots. The future for pilot jobs is hard to predict. Fighter jets that can be flown from the ground without a pilot on board may reduce the need for human pilots. However, people will be needed to control these jets without pilots and to plan how the aircraft will be used.

Fighter pilots have a college degree and officer training. Some people get both at the same time by joining the Reserve Officers' Training Corps (ROTC) in college or by going to college at one of the U.S. military academies. Other people get officer training after college.

Once you are a military officer, you can apply for fighter pilot training. There is no guarantee that there will be an opening.

If you are eager to start preparing, you can learn a sport to keep fit and study English, math, and science. Who knows—in a decade or two you may be pulling 9 Gs as you bank out of a nose dive.

Answer Key

Pages 4-5: Air Acrobatics:
The aircraft is at 6 o'clock. If you are in the center of the clock facing 12 o'clock, then 6 o'clock is behind you.

Pages 6-7: Fighter Pilot Gear:
The G force is 3 times greater than a roller coaster's G force. Find *roller coaster* in the table. Its G force is 3. What number times 3 equals 9? **3** × 3 G = 9 G Think about this: If Colonel Sanchez weighs 130 pounds, then 9 G would made her feel like she weighs 1,170 pounds; 9 × 130 = 1,170.

Pages 8-9: Helmets and Cockpits:
The hill is 1,080 feet tall. Find the difference between the plane's altitude (1,800 feet) and its height (720 feet). 1,800 − 720 = 1,080.

Pages 10-11: Expensive Machines:
Six Slammers cost $2,316,000. Find the cost of one Slammer in the table: $386,000. Add six $386 thousands or multiply 6 × $386,000.

Pages 12-13: Air Force Fighter Planes:
The range is 1,030 miles greater than the combat radius, or more than twice the combat radius. You might expect the range to be exactly twice the combat radius, but combat missions can require more fuel than across-country flights, depending on the mission or threat. Pilots may fly faster or slower to approach targets, and they have to turn away from the targets.

Pages 14-15: Marine Fighter Planes:
Here is one way to do it. The scissors were rotated on the red bolt.

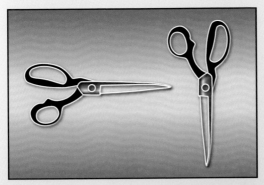

Pages 16-17: Navy Fighter Planes:
1,000 feet. To find how many feet are in 290 yards, you can multiply 290 and 3, or you can add 290 three times. But do you really need to find an exact answer? Round 290 to 300. Three 3 hundreds is 900.

Pages 18-19: Fueling an Aircraft:
3,000 gallons. Divide 18,000 by 6. You can use a basic fact: 18 thousands ÷ 6 = 3 thousands, or 3,000.

Pages 20-21: In-Flight Fueling:
2 minutes. Divide 13,000 by 6,500. Or see how many times you can subtract 6,500 from 13,000. You can subtract 6,500 two times.

Pages 22-23: Supersonic:
At 20,000 feet you have to be traveling at a speed greater than 707 miles per hour to be supersonic. 700 miles per hour isn't fast enough. At 30,000 feet, 700 miles per hour is a supersonic speed. It's faster than the speed of sound at 30,000 feet, which is 678 miles per hour.

Pages 24-25: Stealth:
Surfaces at a right angle to you would bounce your radio waves back to you. Examples of surfaces that might be at a right angle to you are a wall, a computer screen, a door, and the side of a box.

Pages 26-27: Navigation:
1,000 nautical miles. A nautical mile is greater than a standard mile. So, 1,000 nautical miles is greater than 1,000 standard miles. If you wanted to, you could figure out that 1,000 nautical miles (abbreviated nmi) are equivalent to 1,150 standard miles: 1,000 nmi × 1.15 mi = 1,150 mi.

Glossary

agile—Easy to turn or maneuver; sometimes said of an aircraft.

aircraft carrier—A large military ship that carries planes and has a runway on its deck.

altimeter—An instrument that displays **altitude** or **height**.

altitude—Distance above sea level.

beacon—A light used as a signal.

catapult—A device that works something like a giant slingshot to give a plane the speed it needs to take off from an **aircraft carrier**.

circumference—The distance around a circle.

compass—A device for showing direction.

G force—A measure of how heavy a person feels.

hangar—A large building where planes are kept.

height—Distance from an object on Earth's surface to an aircraft above.

hover—To float in one place in the air.

lift—A force that moves a plane upward when its wings move through air.

Mach—The ratio of an object's speed to the speed of sound.

nautical mile—A unit of length used by pilots and sailors; 1 nautical mile is about 1.15 standard (statute) miles.

perpendicular—At a **right angle**. The line segments in a capital T are perpendicular.

radar—A system that sends and receives radio waves to locate objects.

radius—A line segment that goes from the center to the outside of a circle.

right angle—An angle equal to 90 degrees.

sonic booms—A pair of loud booms caused by an aircraft traveling faster than the speed of sound.

stealthy—Hard to notice or detect.

strobe light—A light that flashes over and over again.

supersonic—Faster than the speed of sound.

terrain—The natural features of an area of land, including such things as hills, streams, and rocks.

transfer fuel—Fuel on a tanker aircraft used for fueling planes in flight.

visor—The clear part of a helmet that protects a pilot's face.

To Learn More

Read these books:

Duble, Kathleen Benner. *Pilot Mom*. Watertown, Mass.: Charlesbridge, 2003.

Old, Wendie. *To Fly: The Story of the Wright Brothers*. New York: Clarion, 2002.

Osborn, Shane. *Born to Fly: The Heroic Story of Downed U.S. Navy Pilot Lt. Shane Osborn*. New York: Delacorte Press, 2001.

Tarpley, Natasha. *Joe-Joe's First Flight*. New York: Knopf, 2003.

Look up these Web sites:

NASA, Aviation Navigation Tutorial
http://www.virtualskies.arc.nasa.gov/navigation/tutorial/tutorial1.html

PBS, "Battle of the X-Planes"
http://www.pbs.org/wgbh/nova/xplanes

Smithsonian Institution, National Air and Space Museum
http://www.nasm.si.edu

U.S. Air Force, Interactive Fighter Jet Facts and Videos
http://www.airforce.com

Key Internet search terms:

aircraft, fighter jet, G force

Index

About the Author

Mary Hense has always loved planes and spaceships. When she was a girl, she and her brother Jim built model planes. As a Girl Scout, she gave talks about constellations at a planetarium. Now, after developing textbooks for more than 30 years, Hense enjoys air shows and NASA exhibits. From her backyard in Florida, she can see rockets take off from the Kennedy Space Center, which is more than 60 miles away!